Copyright © 2020 All rights re

This eBook is a copyright material and must not be replicated, recreated, moved, dispersed, rented, authorized or freely performed or utilized in any capacity with the exception of as explicitly allowed recorded as a hard copy by the distributers, as permitted under the terms and conditions under which it was bought or as carefully allowed by pertinent copyright law. Any unapproved circulation or utilization of this content might be an immediate encroachment of the creator's and distributer's privileges, and those dependable might be at risk in law as needs are.

Contents

Copyright © 2020 All rights reserved 1

This eBook is a copyright material and must not be replicated, recreated, moved, dispersed, rented, authorized or freely performed or utilized in any capacity with the exception of as explicitly allowed recorded as a hard copy by the distributers, as permitted under the terms and conditions under which it was bought or as carefully allowed by pertinent copyright law. Any unapproved circulation or utilization of this content might be an immediate encroachment of the creator's and distributer's privileges, and those dependable might be at risk in law as needs are. 1

    Gastric sleeve surgery 6

The Gastric Sleeve Bariatric Cookbook for Beginners: Easy and Nutritional Recipes to Lose Weight Fast and Healthy for Every Stage of Bariatric Surgery Recovery. Manage Your Weight and Start a Better Relationship with Food. 100+ recipes 6

    Introduction 7

    Things to Know About Gastric Sleeve Weight Loss Surgery 8

What exactly does gastric sleeve surgery means? 9

    Is it successful? 10

    Weight reduction benefits 11

    Who's a fantastic candidate for this surgery? 12

    What are the complications and risks? 13

    Other concerns 16

    How can your diet alter following gastric sleeve surgery? 17

    Dietary changes 18

    The Main Point 20

    Long-Term Infection after Gastric Sleeve Surgery 22

    Risks vs. Rewards 22

    Gastric Sleeve vs. Bypass vs. Banding 23

    Listed below are two key long-term factors to maintain Head: 24

    • Weight and Nutrition 24

    • Failure to eliminate 25

    • Regain 25

    • Nutritional Shortfalls 25

    • Food Intolerance 26

- Physical Symptoms 27
- Dyspepsia 27
- Nausea 27
- Diarrhea 28
- Sagging Skin Care 28
- Medical Problems 29
- Persistence of Chronic Conditions 29
- Gastroesophageal Reflux Disease (GERD) 29
- Stomach Ulcers 29
- Gallstones 30
- Stomach Obstruction 30
- Abdominal Adhesions 30
- Abscess 31
- Delayed Leak 31
- Incisional Hernia 31
- Psychological or Social Concerns 32
- Addiction Transfer 32
- Divorce 32
- A Word By Verywell 33

Chapter 2 recipes for gastric sleeve 34
    Weight Management & Bariatrics 37
    Chicken Caprese 40
    Black Bean and Corn Salad 43
    Five Creative Approaches to Flavor Water 46

Basil and Blueberries 47

Cucumber and Mint 47

Watermelon 47

Strawberries and Sugar-free Lemonade 48

Infused Ice Cubes... 48

Peanut Applesauce Chicken 49

Spicy Peanut Vegetarian Chili....................................... 51

Peanut Butter and Jelly Pancakes................................. 55

Peanut Powder Salad Dressing..................................... 57

Pumpkin-Ricotta Protein Pie 60

High-Protein Pumpkin Pie Oatmeal 64

Apple and Tuna Sandwiches Recipe 66

Baked Chicken with Vegetables.................................... 69

Silky Chocolate Soy Dessert Recipe 72

Pork and Black Bean Verde Stew Recipe...................... 76

Asian Chicken Lettuce Wraps Recipe 79

Chicken Cheesesteak Wrap Recipe............................... 84

Not Truly Fried Rice Recipe 87

Egg-Chilada Recipe.. 92

Cheesecake Pudding Recipe... 95

Pan-Fried Rainbow Trout Recipe 96

Pumpkin and Black Bean Soup Recipe 98

Asian Pork Tenderloin Recipe..................................... 102

Greek Yogurt Chicken Recipe 105

High-Protein Cottage Cheese Pancakes Recipe 107

Spicy Deviled Eggs Recipe 110

Slow-Cooker Chicken Taco Filling Recipe 113

Ginger Beef Stir Fry Recipe 115

Classic Hummus Recipe 119

Chapter 2 Cosmetic Surgery Gains besides Helping You Shed Weight 121

Dietary alterations after bariatric surgery 122

Weight reduction Just One health benefit of several 123

What's a sleeve gastrectomy? 125

Why is this surgery the favored choice by a lot of? 126

What are the advantages? 126

How long does the surgery take and how quickly is the Retrieval? 127

Is there some particular follow up required? 127

What Type of weight reduction can you expect out of a sleeve Gastrectomy and can it be lasting? 129

Which Are the Most Common Post-Op Risks and Side Effects Connected with Cosmetic Surgery? 129

Summary of Bariatric Surgery Risks and Complications by Process 131

Reduce Your Bariatric Surgery Hazards 135

What's recovery following surgery like? 136

What can you expect in your short term recovery? 136

Request assistance if you need it 137

Practice your new eating plan 137

Give yourself time before resuming normal activities.....139

Work through short term emotional Results 140

Think about your long-term healing? 140

Stick with your new eating plan 141

Get busy 142

Take vitamins and nutritional supplements....................142

Meet with a dietitian 143

Maintain your followup appointments with your Physician 144

Prepare yourself for longer-term psychological Results..144

Conclusion 146

Gastric sleeve surgery

The Gastric Sleeve Bariatric Cookbook for Beginners: Easy and Nutritional Recipes to Lose Weight Fast and Healthy for Every Stage of Bariatric Surgery Recovery. Manage Your Weight and Start a Better Relationship with Food. 100+ recipes

Introduction

Sleeve Gastrectomy is a procedure where the left side of the gut (higher curvature) is removed. This can be a restrictive bariatric surgery. The Sleeve Gastrectomy doesn't demand some "rerouting" or reconnecting of their intestines. It's often easier than the RNY gastric bypass. It doesn't require implantation of a device like the Adjustable Gastric Band. The surgeons in Virginia Mason specialize in gastric bypass surgery. This surgery balances threat of operation together with long-term weight reduction and long-term health complications better than some of those choices. Both the laparoscopic and open approaches to weight loss surgery create similar long-term outcomes. The open approach is usually associated with an extended recovery period. Revisional weight reduction surgery is done to alter or repair a preexisting surgery for treatment of morbid obesity. While bariatric surgery provides results for most individuals, many patients -- especially people who might have experienced an outmoded surgery performed several years ago -- might not have experienced the favorable outcome they anticipated. Other individuals experience significant side effects or complications in past weight reduction surgery that's affecting their quality of life. Revisional weight reduction surgery might require the open strategy.

Things to Know About Gastric Sleeve Weight Loss Surgery

1 approach to tackle obesity would be with regular surgery. This Kind of surgery involves removing or diminishing the size of your tummy. Bariatric surgery typically results in rapid weight reduction.

Gastric sleeve surgery is one of several Kinds of bariatric Surgery choices. Medical professionals typically call it vertical sleeve gastrectomy.

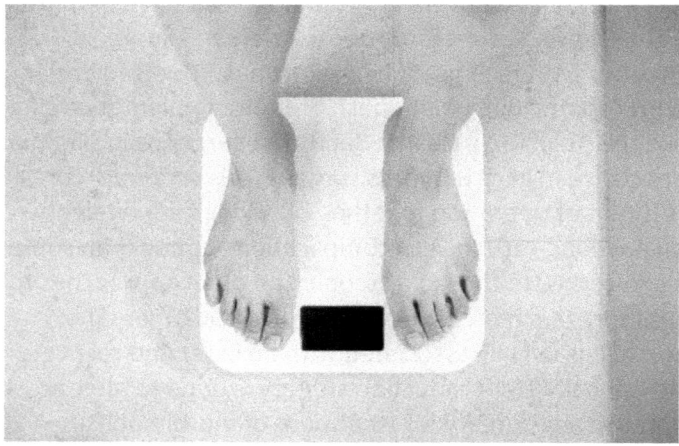

In this Guide, you'll have a closer look at what is involved in gastric sleeve surgery, such as its efficacy and potential complications.

What exactly does gastric sleeve surgery means?

Gastric sleeve surgery is almost always performed as a invasive procedure using a laparoscope. This usually means a very long, thin tube is inserted into your abdomen through several tiny incisions. This tube has a light and a small camera attached to it and many tools.

Gastric sleeve surgery is performed with general anesthesia, which is medication that puts you right into a really deep sleep and takes a ventilator to breathe for you during the surgery.

The surgery involves dividing your gut into 2 unequal Components. Approximately 80 percent of those outer curved portion of your gut is cut off and removed.

The advantages of the remaining 20 percent are then stapled or sutured together. This produces a banana-shaped stomach that is just about 25% of its initial size.

You are going to be at the living room about one hour. After the Surgery is finished, you're going to be moved into the recovery area for health care. You are going to be at the recovery area for one more hour or so as you awaken in the anesthesia.

The tiny incisions in your abdomen typically cure fast. The minimally invasive nature of this surgery makes it possible to recuperate faster than a process where your stomach is started using a bigger incision.

Unless there are complications, you should have the Ability to go Home within two or three days following the surgery.

Is it successful?

Gastric sleeve surgery helps you Drop weight in two manners:

• Your gut Is considerably smaller in order to feel full and stop eating earlier. As a result, that you take in fewer calories.

• The component Of the stomach that generates ghrelin -- a hormone that is connected with appetite -- has been eliminated, which means you are much less hungry.

According to the American Society of Metabolic and Allergic Surgery, you can expect to lose at least 50 per cent of your extra weight over the 18 to 24 weeks after gastric sleeve surgery. Some folks lose 60 to 70 percent .

It is Important to Keep in Mind that this Is Only Going to happen if you Are dedicated to adhering to the diet and exercise plan recommended by the physician. By embracing these lifestyle modifications, you are more inclined to keep the weight off long term.

Weight reduction benefits

Losing a significant Number of excess weights can improve your quality of life also make it less difficult to carry out many daily tasks.

Another important advantage of weight reduction is the lower hazard Of obesity-related wellness conditions. These include:

- Type 2 diabetes

- Significant cholesterol (hyperlipidemia)

- Significant Blood pressure (hypertension)

- Obstructive Sleep apnea

Who's a fantastic candidate for this surgery?

Bariatric surgery of any type, such as gastric sleeve Surgery, is just considered a choice when powerful attempts to boost your diet and exercise habits, and also the usage of weight-loss drugs, have not worked.

Even after that, you have to meet specific standards to be eligible for A regular procedure. These standards are based on the own body mass index (BMI) and if you have some obesity-related wellness conditions.

Qualifying conditions:

• Intense (morbid) obesity (BMI rating of 40 or greater)

• Obesity (BMI rating of 35 to 39) with one important obesity-related condition

Sometimes, gastric sleeve surgery is completed if you are Obese but do not fulfill the standards for obesity, however, you get a substantial health condition associated with your weight.

What are the complications and risks?

Gastric sleeve surgery is regarded as a relatively safe procedure. But like all significant surgeries, there may be dangers and complications.

Some complications may happen after any surgery. All these include:

• Hemorrhage. Bleeding in the wound or within your body may result in shock when it is intense.

- Deep vein thrombosis (DVT). Surgery as well as the healing procedure can boost your chance of a blood clot forming on your vein, usually in a leg vein.

- Pulmonary embolism. A pulmonary embolism can occur when a part of a blood clot breaks off and travels to your lungs.

- Irregular heartbeat. Surgery may boost the danger of an irregular pulse, particularly atrial fibrillation.

- Pneumonia. Pain can permit you to take shallow breaths that may cause a lung disease, such as pneumonia.

Gastric sleeve surgery may have added complications. A few possible side effects that are specific to this surgery include:

- Gastric leaks. Stomach fluids can flow in the suture line on your gut where it had been stitched back together.

- Stenosis. Section of your gastric sleeve may shut, resulting in an obstruction in your stomach.

- Vitamin deficiencies. The part of your gut that is eliminated is partially responsible for the absorption of vitamins that your body needs. If you don't take vitamin supplements, then this may result in deficiencies.

- Heartburn (GERD). Reshaping your gut can cause or aggravate heartburn. This may normally be treated with over-the-counter drugs.

It is Important to Keep in Mind that changing your diet and Exercise habits are crucial to losing the weight and keeping it off following gastric sleeve surgery. It is potential to gain the weight back if you

- eat also much

- consume an unhealthy diet

- exercise too little

Other concerns

Another Frequent concern, especially Once You Eliminate a Good Deal of Weight fast, is that the massive number of surplus skin you might be left with as the pounds drop away. This is a frequent complication of gastric sleeve surgery.

This excess skin could be removed if it disturbs you. But remember it may take around 18 months for the body to stabilize following gastric sleeve surgery. That is why it's generally better to wait until considering a skin removal process. Until then, you might want to try out some strategies for tightening loose skin.

Another thing to think about before choosing to have gastric Sleeve surgery is that, unlike any other regular surgeries, gastric sleeve surgery is permanent. If you aren't satisfied with the outcome, your tummy cannot be transformed back to how it was.

How can your diet alter following gastric sleeve surgery?

Before gastric sleeve surgery is completed, you typically must consent to particular lifestyle modifications recommended by your physician. These changes are supposed to assist you reach and maintain weight loss.

One of these changes involves eating a healthy diet for the remainder of your life.

Your physician will recommend the very best gastric sleeve diet to get you after your surgery. The dietary modifications your surgeon proposes may be like the overall dietary guidelines under.

Dietary changes

• Two weeks Prior surgery. Boost protein, reduced carbohydrates, and remove sugar from the dietplan.

• Two days Prior to and the first week following surgery. Ingest only clear fluids which are caffeine- and - carbonation-free.

• For the Next three months. It's possible to add pureed food into your dietplan.

You will usually have the Ability to eat regular, Healthful food about 1 month following your surgery. You might discover that you just eat less than prior to the process since you will get full fast and will not feel overly hungry.

Your restricted diet and smaller foods may cause some Nutritional deficiencies. It is important to compensate for this by choosing multivitamins, calcium supplements, a monthly B-12 shot, and many others as recommended by your physician.

In accordance with the Centers of Medicare & Medicare Services (CMS), Medicare will cover gastric sleeve surgery if you meet the following requirements:

• Your BMI Is 35 or greater

• You've one or more obesity-related health ailments

• You had been not able to eliminate the weight by simply modifying your diet and exercise habits or simply by taking drugs

Medicare does not cover gastric sleeve surgery in case you are Obese but do not possess an obesity-related health state.

Without health insurance policy, the price of gastric Sleeve surgery may vary widely from 1 area into another, and also from 1 centre to another in the exact same geographical location. Normally, the price could range from $15,000 to over $25,000.

Given this wide variation, it is Ideal to study and Speak to Several operative and surgeons facilities to find one you are comfortable with -- and also one which satisfies your budget.

The Main Point

Gastric sleeve surgery is one of several Kinds of bariatric Surgery choices. It works by making your stomach smaller so that you eat less. Since the dimensions of the gut are reduced, you will also realize that you are less hungry.

To be eligible for gastric sleeve surgery, you need to meet specific criteria. You have to show that you have attempted other weight-loss strategies -- such as diet, exercise, and weight loss drugs -- with no success. Other qualifying standards comprise your BMI and if you have some obesity-related wellness conditions.

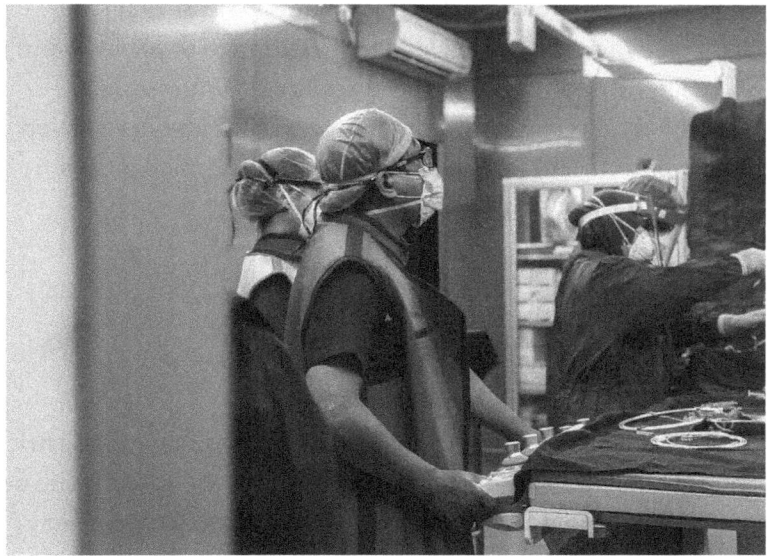

Should you follow a healthy diet and exercise regimen frequently after gastric sleeve surgery, you could have the ability to shed more than 50 per cent of your extra fat within 24 weeks.

However, as with the Majority of surgical procedures, there's the danger of side effects and complications. If you are considering gastric sleeve surgery, speak to your physician about whether you are eligible for this process and if it is a secure solution for you.

Long-Term Infection after Gastric Sleeve Surgery

Gastric sleeve surgery, also called a sleeve gastrectomy, removes about 80 percent of their gut to promote weight reduction. Apart from the dangers inherent with any surgery, gastric sleeve surgery could lead to a vast range of physical and psychological health issues. Those associated with fat and nourishment directly stem from how the rest, tube-like section of the stomach can only hold about 4 oz or 120 milliliters--a substantial reduction from its regular capability.1

Risks vs. Rewards

The remarkable decrease in belly size which results from Gastric sleeve surgery means you may only consume about half a cup at a time (at least initially). Since the quantity of food which may be consumed is limited, the amount calorie which may be obtained in is diminished. This is what contributes to weight reduction.

Gastric sleeve surgery is irreversible and May Lead to positive Health results for obese men and women who've fought with achieving and maintaining weight loss. And general, gastric sleeve is deemed secure when compared to other commonly performed surgeries.

Deaths from the procedure are rare, and if done by a qualified physician, the surgery has minimum complications. Nevertheless, when they do occur, complications may range from minor annoyances to important and possibly life-altering troubles.

Severe complications are those that occur shortly afterwards surgery. They include pain, bleeding, antastamotic flows (from the links between the intestines), and blood clots.2 the chronic issues detailed here are long-term, which means that they appear or persist six months following the onset of surgery.

Surgery is a tool, not a magic bullet. It requires you to follow release directions, limit food consumption, and adhere to the program supplied by your physician. It's likely to overeat and possess minimum weight reduction after surgery. It's also likely to have a severe complication either because of inadequate adherence for your post-surgical strategy or the surgery itself.

Gastric Sleeve vs. Bypass vs. Banding

There are various kinds of bariatric surgery, of which Gastric sleeve is merely one. There are lots of differences between these, and you need to examine each these options with your physician prior to deciding a process so you are able to guarantee that what you select would be the ideal alternative for you.

Listed below are two key long-term factors to maintain Head:

- A gastric sleeve is permanent. Contrary to the gastric band process --in which the ring that "cinches" the gut to split it into two pouches may be eliminated if There's a difficulty --that the portion of the gut removed together with the sleeve process Can't Be substituted if there are issues or complications with digestion.3

- You will not shed as much weight using a gastric sleeve. While individuals who have gastric bypass surgery generally shed weight and maintain a greater proportion of extra weight long term in comparison with people who have gastric sleeve surgery, skip can present its own set of hard long-term troubles.

- **Weight and Nutrition**

- While the Goal of gastric sleeve surgery would be to encourage weight loss, there's a possibility you cannot drop as much as expected or you shed weight, but gain it back. What's more, while the decrease in food intake makes it possible to reduce calories, which also means that you're consuming fewer calories --that could cause deficiencies.

• **Failure to eliminate**

• That is a Serious problem in which the surgery is unsuccessful for weight reduction. The pouch might be too big, the individual may dismiss discharge directions, or a different issue could be found that prevents weight reduction.5

• **Regain**

• From the First days following the surgery, the stomach pouch that remains is quite little and will hold approximately half a cup of food at the same time. With time, the pouch stretches and can accommodate larger quantities of food in a single sitting. This dilation allows bigger meals to be absorbed and may eventually lead to weight reduction weight or stopping reduction beginning.5

• Losing Weight after surgery simply to acquire all of back it normally begins in the next year following surgery, if it happens at all. Bariatric processes are a excellent tool for weight reduction, but if customs aren't altered and preserved, it's likely to acquire some or all the surplus weight again.5

• **Nutritional Shortfalls**

• Unlike Many gastric bypass surgeries, patients that have a gastric sleeve process don't have any change in their capacity to consume nutrients in the gut. On the other hand, the remarkable drop in food intake may result in problems in taking in sufficient nourishment. Problems such as nausea and diarrhea may also lead to problems with consuming enough nutrients and calories also.

- In such Cases, a perfect whole-foods diet might not be sufficient to provide all the requirements of their human anatomy.5 because malnutrition can be extremely severe, your physician may suggest using vitamin and mineral supplements, medicine, and other interventions to keep you long-term.6

- **Food Intolerance**

- One of The advantages of a gastric sleeve is the fact that all foods may be consumed after the process; other bariatric surgeries need you to avoid particular foods. But, that doesn't mean that the body will endure all kinds of foods.

- A 2018 Study discovered that food tolerance diminished after perpendicular sleeve gastrectomy, especially in regards to foods such as red meat, rice, pasta, and bread. The researchers noticed that this is probably because of the physiological and anatomical alterations in limiting the quantity of food that you can consume at the same time.7

- **Physical Symptoms**

- Some Patients can experience gastrointestinal difficulties as a complication of gastric sleeve surgery. Although these may seem immediately after surgery, some patients might experience them for an elongated period of time. Sagging skin could be an additional complication which you experience after surgery.

- **Dyspepsia**

- Indigestion, Or an upset stomach, may be more regular following gastric sleeve surgery.8 this might be a result of the decreased volume of the gut and changes in how food goes through your gut and intestines.9

- **Nausea**

- Nausea is among the more prevalent issues that individuals face after sleeve gastrectomy.10 For many, this enhances after recovering from surgery, but for many others, the issue persists for weeks or long term.

- While it is not clear what causes nausea in this event, it can be partially as a result of food staying on your stomach for longer lengths of time.11 Nausea drugs can be found, which might be useful for many.

- Diarrhea

- For a few Patients, nausea is a severe issue that may persist following gastric sleeve surgery.12 this may happen for any range of reasons, such as alterations in gut microbiota and accelerated exposure to the small gut to undigested nutrients.13

- In instances that Last for a protracted period of time, the physician or even a gastroenterologist may have the ability to help stop nausea, which may cause malnutrition and dehydration.

- Signs You Are Dehydrated

- Sagging Skin Care

- This Complication is typical with all kinds of weight loss surgeries and can be caused by skin stretching throughout the time of obesity.14 A panniculectomy could possibly be an choice to get rid of extra skin, but many surgeons prefer to wait till the patient's weight has been steady for one or two years before removing extra skin.

- Medical Problems

- Gastric Sleeve surgery may cause medical conditions which range from moderate to severe. Speak to your physician if you have any worries about your probability of developing a health dilemma after surgery.

- Persistence of Chronic Conditions

- For a few, Eliminating chronic health problems--diabetes, hypertension, and many others --is your reason behind getting this surgery. Sometimes, these issues do not disappear after surgery, or else they might go away briefly from the first months or years following surgery and return afterwards.

- Gastroesophageal Reflux Disease (GERD)

- Heartburn, alongside other signs of GERD (bloating, feelings of fullness, and upset stomach), is common following this surgery and frequently requires medicine.5

- Stomach Ulcers

- Stomach Ulcers, called peptic ulcersare far more prevalent after gastric sleeve surgery and therefore are generally diagnosed through an upper endoscopy following the individual experiences bleeding (viewed as a dark, tarry feces or as blood in vomit) or pain in the gut area.15

• Gallstones

• Gallstones Are more prevalent following all kinds of bariatric surgery, building a cholecystectomy (surgery to remove the stomach) more prevalent to weight loss surgery patients.16

• Stomach Obstruction

• Scarring And narrowing of the outlet of the gut, also called stenosis, may make it hard or perhaps impossible to digest food.17 This complication is normally repaired by means of a physician that "stretches" or fixes the region which has been narrowed.

• Abdominal Adhesions

• The organs And cells of the gut are obviously slippery, letting them slide past each other through movements like bending, bending, and walking. After surgery, scarring may make these cells "stay" to each other. This induces a pulling sensation that can range from bothersome to debilitating with motion.18 Abdominal adhesions may also result in small bowel obstructions.

• Abscess

• An Abscess is a collection of infectious material (pus) that creates from the entire body in a pocket-like location. This typically happens soon after the initial surgery, because of spillage or leakage of intestinal contents. In the case of gastric sleeve surgery, abscesses have been diagnosed from the spleen, a few necessitating the manhood to be removed, but this Is Quite uncommon.19

• Delayed Leak

• Most suture Line flows, also referred to as suture line disruption or SLD, and are found shortly after surgery. Sometimes, however, the region of the gut which was stitched together will start to flow months or years following surgery.

• These Later leaks are a lot milder but may be both annoying, and they might require drugs, hospitalization, or surgery to fix.20

• Incisional Hernia

• A hernia can form at the website of any surgical incision. This danger is lessened by minimally invasive (laparoscopic) surgical methods, but a hernia may still form in the months and years after this type of process. Normally, that looks like a little bulge in the Website of a surgical incision.21

• Psychological or Social Concerns

• Gastric Sleeve surgery can change your mental and psychological well-being, in addition to your relationships with other people. While weighing possible physical complications of this process is vital, these should not be overlooked.

• Addiction Transfer

• That is a Phenomenon occurring to some people when they're not able to work with food as a means to self-medicate their feelings.22 by way of instance, after a difficult day on the job, it's not feasible to go home and binge an whole container of ice cream--it simply won't match in the gut.

• Additional Kinds of addictions become more attractive since they're still possible using the bigger gut size--alcohol misuse, drug abuse, and sexual dependence being one of the very frequent after surgery.

• Divorce

- From the United States, an average of 50 percent of marriages end in divorce; a few sources show that the speed of divorce following bariatric surgeries is as large as 80 percent.

- A 2018 Study indicated that divorce levels following gastric sleeve surgery might increase because the remarkable weight loss that impacts may impact the dynamics of a connection. This could occur if a spouse feels envious or no longer desired.

- Patients who are thinking about the surgery are advised to speak to their spouses about any possible problems and how they may handle anxieties should they appear.23 Couples might reap having this dialog with the assistance of a therapist.

A Word By Verywell

- One of The critical criteria that research scientists consider when assessing the success and security of operations is 10-year results. In cases like this, when it comes to the way patients maintain weight loss, what their general health resembles, and some other complications they've had because of surgery.

- It's Important to understand that gastric sleeve surgery is a fairly new process, so there's less 10-year information for gastric sleeve surgery than there is with other surgeries.

Therefore, more long-term complications may be added to the listing later on.

Chapter 2 recipes for gastric sleeve

Bariatric Surgery Recipes

Yogurt Breakfast Popsicles

Weight Management & Bariatrics

SERVINGS: 6

Prep time: 5 minutes

Freeze time: 4 hours

INGREDIENTS

1 cup Greek yogurt, plain, non-fat

1/2 cup milk 1 percent or skim

1/2 cup regular or instant vanilla

1 cup mixed berries or sliced veggies

DIRECTIONS

1. Mix together the yogurt and milk.

2. Split the mix between your Popsicle molds.

3. Put a Couple berries to each mould.

4. Split that the 1/2 cup oatmeal one of every mould.

5. Put a Wooden ice cream stick into each mould and put the popsicles to the freezer for at least 4 hours prior to eating.

6. To eliminate the popsicles, run the mound below a small hot water till they come loose.

NUTRITIONAL VALUES

Serving size: 1 Popsicle

Calories: 75

Fat: 0.6 g

Cholesterol: 3 mg

Sodium: 36 mg

Carbohydrates: 11 g

Dietary Fiber: 1.5 g

Sugar: 4 g

Protein: 5 g

Shrimp Ceviche

Weight Management & Bariatrics

SERVINGS: 4

Prep time: 25 minutes

INGREDIENTS

1 pound medium raw shrimp

1 cup lime juice (roughly 5 new limes)

4 medium tomatoes (Roma or Italian), diced OR 8 oz Canned, diced tomatoes

1 small red onion, peeled, finely chopped (roughly 3/4 Cup chopped)

1 bunch cilantro, stemmed and thinly sliced

2 serrano chili peppers, seeds and ribs removed, minced (optional)

Suggestion: To get a light option, attempt half a medium green bell pepper.

DIRECTIONS

1. In a Bowl, combine fish and lime juice.

2. Cover and Marinate for approximately 10 to 15 minutes or until colour changes to pink. Don't worry too long, since the fish is going to "overcook" and toughen.

3. Insert Onions, celery, tomatoes, chili peppers and cilantro.

4. Gradually stir to blend.

5. Season with salt to taste.

6. Drink Chilly.

NUTRITIONAL VALUES

Serving size: 4 oz

Calories: 160

Fat: 1 g

Cholesterol: 220 mg

Sodium: 265 mg

Carbohydrates: 13 g

Dietary Fiber: 2 g

Sugar: 5 g

Protein: 25 g

Chicken Caprese

Weight Management & Bariatrics

SERVINGS: 4

Prep time: 20 minutes

INGREDIENTS

1 lb boneless, skinless chicken breasts

1 tbsp olive oil

1 tsp dry Italian seasoning (or equivalent portions of garlic Powder, dried oregano and dried ginger)

4 thick (1/2-inch) slices ripe tomato

4 1-ounce pieces fresh mozzarella cheese

3 tbsp balsamic vinegar

2 tbsp thinly sliced ginger

Pepper to taste

DIRECTIONS

1. Heat a Grill or skillet over medium heat.

2. Drizzle 1 Tbsp of olive oil on chicken breasts and season to taste and pepper.

3. Sprinkle Italian seasoning over the chicken.

4. Set the Chicken on the grill and cook 3 to 5 minutes each side, or until done. Cook time will change based upon the depth of your chicken breasts.

5. When Chicken is done, top with a piece of mozzarella cheese and cook for 1 minute.

6. Eliminate from heat and place chicken breasts on a plate.

7. Top each Breast with a single piece of tomato, thinly chopped ginger and pepper to taste.

8. Drizzle with balsamic vinegar or balsamic glaze and function.

NUTRITIONAL VALUES

Serving size: 6 oz (4 oz chicken with 1 oz tomato and one ounce cheese)

Calories: 230

Fat: 9 g

Cholesterol: 80 mg

Sodium: 105 mg

Carbohydrates: 4 g

Dietary Fiber: 0 g

Sugar: 2.5 g

Protein: 33 g

Black Bean and Corn Salad

Weight Management & Bariatrics

SERVINGS: 6

INGREDIENTS

1 cup corn, whole kernel

2 cans (16-ounces each) black beans, rinsed and drained

1/4 cup chopped, chopped fresh

2 tbsp red onion, minced

1/4 cup

2 tbsp olive oil

1 tsp lemon juice

1 tsp garlic, minced

1 tsp honey or brown sugar

Dash salt

1/4 teaspoon ground black pepper

DIRECTIONS

1. Mix new Walnut, black beans, red onion and fresh parsley together in a large mixing bowl.

2. Whisk Together balsamic vinegar, olive oil, lemon juice, honey, garlic, pepper and salt.

3. Pour Black beans and corn mix.

4. Let the Salad marinade for 30 minutes prior to serving.

NUTRITIONAL VALUES

Serving size: 1/2 cup

Calories: 160

Fat: 5 g

Cholesterol: 0 mg

Potassium: 306 mg

Sodium: 40 mg

Carbohydrates: 23 g

Dietary Fiber: 6 g

Sugars: 3 g

Protein: 6 g

Five Creative Approaches to Flavor Water

Weight Management & Bariatrics

Water in the summertime is much more significant than ever. Due to the summer heat, we've got a inclination to sweat more and also lose more water during our breath. The best way to avoid dehydration is to drink even if you aren't thirsty. Thirst might be a indication that you're dried.

Basil and Blueberries

Rinse blueberries and basil under cool running water. Crush Blueberries and set to a water pitcher. Leave the basil onto the sprig and then increase the water. Let me sit for a couple hours in the fridge. The longer it sits, the larger the taste. The infused water may keep up to 3 times and you'll probably reuse the fruit by adding additional water into the pitcher.

Cucumber and Mint

Scrub the skillet and mint under cool running water. Thinly slice the cucumbers and set to a water pitcher. The larger the surface area of the cucumbers, the faster the water is going to be flavored. Leave the mint on the sprig and then increase the water. Let me sit for a couple hours in the fridge. The longer it sits, the larger the taste. The infused water may keep up to 3 times and you'll probably reuse the fruit by adding additional water into the pitcher.

Watermelon

Cube the carrot and set to a water pitcher. The Higher the surface area of the fruit, the faster the water is going to be flavored. Leave the mint on the sprig and then increase the water. Let me sit for a couple hours in the fridge. The longer it sits, the larger the taste. The infused water may keep up to 3 times and you'll probably reuse the fruit by adding additional water into the pitcher.

Strawberries and Sugar-free Lemonade

Rinse strawberries under cool running water. With a cheese Grater, grate the berries to a water pitcher. Squirt at several drops of sugar free lemonade. You can use products such as Crystal Light or Dasani Drops. For another choice it is possible to add finely chopped lemons rather. Let me sit for a couple hours in the fridge. The longer it sits, the larger the taste. The infused water may keep up to 3 times and you'll probably reuse the fruit by adding additional water into the pitcher.

Infused Ice Cubes

Seeking to keep cool? Insert any nicely cut herb and fruit mixture straight to a ice cube tray. Pour boiling water; let cooling before putting it in the freezer. By heating up the water before freezing itpenetrates the fruit, vegetable, or herb to discharge the yummy aromatic chemical --providing you the maximum amount of taste from every cube.

Peanut Applesauce Chicken

Weight Management & Bariatrics

SERVINGS: 8

Prep time: 10 minutes

Cook time: 1 hour

INGREDIENTS

Two 1/2 pounds chicken pieces

1/4 cup yellow mustard

⅛ cup Splenda brown sugarunpacked

1/2 cup roasted peanuts

Salt and pepper to taste

1 (15 oz) jar applesauce, unsweetened

DIRECTIONS

1. Cook Poultry in sauté pan.

2. After Nearing entirely cooked, add applesauce, mustard, brown sugar and powdered peanuts.

3. Stir Ingredients together.

4. Simmer Over moderate heat until an internal temperature of 165ºF is attained.

NUTRITIONAL VALUES

Serving size: 2 tbsp

Calories: 50

Fat: 2 g

Cholesterol: 60 mg

Sodium: 203 mg

Carbohydrates: 13 g

Dietary Fiber: 2 g

Sugar: 10 g

Protein: 3 g

Spicy Peanut Vegetarian Chili

Weight Management & Bariatrics

SERVINGS: 10 -- 12

You won't miss the meat in this hearty, satisfying chili, Created with peanuts.

INGREDIENTS

1 tbsp coconut oil (or coconut oil)

1 cup sliced onion

2 tsp garlic, minced

2 tbsp chili powder

1 tsp chipotle chili pepper (optional)

1/4 tsp dried oregano

1 can (16 oz) black beans, drained and rinsed

1 can (16 oz) white beans, drained and rinsed

2/3 cup roasted peanuts

1 can (28 oz) diced tomato

1 can (15 oz) tomato sauce

2 cups vegetable broth

DIRECTIONS

1. In a Large Dutch oven, heat oil on medium heat.

2. Add onion And garlic, sautéing 3 -- 4 minutes until tender.

3. Stir in chili powder, pepper, oregano and salt.

4. Sauté two minutes or until fragrant.

5. Insert Beans, corn, powdered peanuts, tomatoes, tomato soup and sauce.

6. Bring to A boil.

7. Reduce Heat and simmer for approximately thirty minutes.

Notice: This recipe could be cooked in toaster for two -- 3 hours.

NUTRITIONAL VALUES

Serving size: 1/2 cup

Calories: 125

Fat: 2.5 g

Sodium: 582 mg

Carbohydrates: 22 g

Dietary Fiber: 1 g

Sugar: 5 g

Protein: 8 g

Peanut Butter and Jelly Pancakes

Weight Management & Bariatrics

SERVINGS: 4

INGREDIENTS

1/2 cup low-fat cottage cheese

1/2 cup instant oatmeal

2 tbsp powdered peanuts

4 large egg whites

1 cup frozen mixed berry mix

DIRECTIONS

1. Put Items In a blender in this sequence: cottage cheese, celery, roasted lettuce and egg whites.

2. Switch on Blender and mix till smooth just like pancake batter.

3. Pour A bowl and fold berry fruit combination.

4. Use Cooking spray skillet. Makes 4 to 7 pancakes based on dimensions.

NUTRITIONAL VALUES

Serving size: 1 pancake

Calories: 90

Fat: 1.5 g

Cholesterol: 1 mg

Sodium: 195 mg

Carbohydrates: 9 g

Dietary Fiber: 1.5 g

Sugar: 1 g

Protein: 10 g

Peanut Powder Salad Dressing

Weight Management & Bariatrics

SERVINGS: 2

This lower-calorie, Asian-inspired peanut dressing created with Powdered peanut butter is excellent as a dipping sauce or salad dressingtable.

INGREDIENTS

2 tbsp powdered peanuts

1 tbsp soy sauce, low sodium

1 tbsp water

⅛ tsp garlic powder

1/4 tsp ground pepper

1/4 tsp Szechuan chili sauce

1 tsp Splenda brown sugar mix

⅛ Teaspoon sesame oil

DIRECTIONS

Combine all ingredients well and serve. Refrigerate any remaining sauce.

NUTRITIONAL VALUES

Serving size: 2 tbsp

Calories: 50

Carbohydrates: 7 g

Sodium: 562 mg

Fat: 2 g

Protein: 3 g

Dietary Fiber: 1 g

Sugar: 5 g

Pumpkin-Ricotta Protein Pie

Weight Management & Bariatrics

SERVINGS: 12

INGREDIENTS

2 cups 100% pure pumpkin puree, roasted, without salt

2 eggs, large

1 cup milk, nonfat (skim milk)

1 cup ricotta cheese, part skim

1/3 cup Truvia for Baking or Splenda Sugar Blend

2 scoops 100 percent Unflavored Whey Protein Isolate (for example BiPro 1 spoonful =~22 g)

1/2 tsp salt

1 tsp cinnamon, ground

1 tsp nutmeg, ground

2 ounce bundle pecan halves

DIRECTIONS

1. Preheat Oven to 350ºF.

2. Spray 9-inch dish dish and 4 small ramekins with non stick spray.

3. Combination Ricotta cheese, eggs and 1/2 cup of milk until smooth, it needs to be liquid-like.

4. Insert Remaining ingredients and mix until smooth.

5. Pour Liquid mixture into salty cooking dish, decorate with pecans on top.

6. Bake for 40 -- 45 minutes or until middle is set and quite solid. It ought not jiggle when completely cooked. The sides and centre should brown and develop to double its size. Should you experience over-browning on top, reduce fever to 325ºF for the rest of the cooking time.

7. Cool for 1 hour prior to cutting. This also allows for the pie growth to repay.

8. Slice Into 12 even pieces using a fresh knife. Wipe the knife between each piece to get a fresh cut.

Suggestion: If you Opt to utilize a crust (like graham cracker, Or normal pie pastry, you'll have to correct the nutrition info and calories upward accordingly.

NUTRITIONAL VALUES

Serving Size: 1 piece of pie after it is cut into 12 bits

Calories: 105

Cholesterol: 33 mg

Carbohydrates: 10 g

Sodium: 151 mg

Fat: 3.5 g

Protein: 6 g

Dietary Fiber: 2 g

Sugar: 8 g

High-Protein Pumpkin Pie Oatmeal

Weight Management & Bariatrics

SERVINGS: 1)

INGREDIENTS

1/3 cup old fashioned oats (30 g)

1/2 cup pumpkin, canned

⅛ tsp cinnamon

Dash ground cloves

Dash ground ginger

1 tsp Truvia baking mix

1/2 cup no salt added 1 percent cottage cheese

DIRECTIONS

1. Blend Oats, lettuce, pumpkin, and simmer in a microwave safe bowl.

2. Microwave On top for 90 minutes.

3. Stir in The cottage cheese.

4. Microwave On high for 60 minutes.

5. Let sit For a few minutes prior to ingestion.

NUTRITIONAL VALUES

Calories: 205

Cholesterol: 3 mg

Carbohydrates: 34 g

Sodium: 312 mg

Fat: 3 g

Protein: 14 g

Dietary Fiber: 1 g

Sugar: 9 g

Apple and Tuna Sandwiches Recipe

Weight Management & Bariatrics

SERVINGS: 3

INGREDIENTS

1 can tuna, packed in water (6.5 oz, drained)

1 apple

1/4 cup yoghurt, low-fat vanilla

1 tsp mustard

1/2 tsp honey

6 slices whole wheat bread

3 lettuces leaves

DIRECTIONS

1. Wash and Peel the apple. Chop it into little pieces.

2. Drain the Water in the can of tuna.

3. Place the tuna, apple, yogurt, mustard, and honey in a medium bowl. Stir well.

4. Spread 1/2 Cup of the carrot mixture onto every 3 pieces of bread.

5. Top each Sandwich using a chopped lettuce leaf and a piece of bread.

NUTRITIONAL VALUES

Serving size: 1/3 of recipe

Calories: 250

Cholesterol: 28 mg

Carbohydrates: 30 g

Sodium: 330 mg

Fat: 2.5 g

Protein: 23 g

Dietary Fiber: 5 g

Sugar: 5.25 g

Baked Chicken with Vegetables

Weight Management & Bariatrics

SERVINGS: 6

INGREDIENTS

4 celery, chopped

6 carrots, sliced

1 large onion, quartered

1 raw, chicken, cut into bits with skin removed

1/2 cup water

1 tsp thyme

1/4 tsp pepper

DIRECTIONS

1. Preheat Oven to 400 degrees.

2. Place Potatoes, onions and carrots in a large skillet.

3. Place Chicken pieces in addition to the veggies.

4. Mix water, thyme and pepper. Pour over chicken and veggies.

5. Spoon Juices over chicken a couple of times during cooking.

6. Bake for 1 hour or longer until browned and tender.

NUTRITIONAL VALUES

Serving size: ⅙ of recipe

Calories: 240

Carbohydrate: 25 g

Sugar: 10 g

Fat: 3.5 g

Protein: 26 g

Sodium: 130 mg

Fiber: 4 g

Silky Chocolate Soy Dessert Recipe

Weight Management & Bariatrics

SERVINGS: 8

Prep Time: 10 minutes

Chill Time: 30 minutes

Total Time: 40 minutes

INGREDIENTS

1 envelope unflavored gelatin

1/4 cup hot water

1 package (1.4 ounce) sugar-free, fat-free chocolate fudge Immediate pudding

1 cup cold skim milk

16 ounces silken tofu

1/2 tsp vanilla extract

1 tbsp cocoa powder (optional)

1/4 tsp peppermint extract (optional)

DIRECTIONS

1. In a Small bowl, combine the hot water and unflavored gelatin. Set aside and allow to company.

2. In a Medium-sized bowl, mix the cold skim milk and instant pudding mixture.

3. Dice the Lettuce into 1/2- to 1-inch cubes and put in bowl with pudding mix. Quickly whisk together to divide the coconut cubes.

4. Insert the Vanilla extract and discretionary cocoa powder and peppermint extract.

5. Spoon the Pudding and kale mixture to a blender or food processor. Blend till smooth. You might have to blend for approximately 5 minutes and hand blend or shake the contents so the engine doesn't stick.

6. After the Mix includes a smoothie-like texture, slowly add the gelatin until well blended and mix again.

7. Pour A glass 8-inch dish, cover and put in fridge for a minimum of 30 minutes to business. The longer it sits, the firmer it will turn into.

8. Cut into Eight parts and love!

NUTRITIONAL VALUES

Serving size: 1/2 cup or 2-inch square

Calories: 56

Carbohydrate: 6 g

Fat: 1 g (0 g saturated)

Protein: 5 g

Cholesterol: 1 milligram

Sodium: 181 mg

Fiber: 0 g

Pork and Black Bean Verde Stew Recipe

Weight Management & Bariatrics

SERVINGS: 4

INGREDIENTS

2 tsp extra-virgin olive oil

1 lb pork loin or tenderloin, trimmed of visible fat and Cut into 1" cubes

11/4 cup sliced onions

3 cloves garlic

2 canned chipotle peppers in adobo sauce, minced and 1 teaspoon adobo sauce

1 tsp ground cumin

1 packet Goya Sazon with coriander & annatto (or comparable seasoning packet)

1 can (14 oz) no salt added chicken broth

1 can (14.5 oz) no salt added diced tomatoes in juice

1 can (14.5 oz) no salt added black beans, drained & rinsed

1 tsp crushed red pepper flakes (optional)

DIRECTIONS

1. In big Pot or Dutch oven, heat olive oil on medium heat.

2. Add pork Cubes and cookstirring occasionally for 4-6 minutes until browned on all sides.

3. Add onion, garlic and cook for 2-3 minutes, or until beginning to soften.

4. Insert Chipotle sauce and peppers, cumin, and seasoning package. Stir to blend.

5. Insert broth, tomatoes, beans and red pepper flakes if desired. Stir to blend well.

6. Bring Stew to a boil then reduce heat to reduce.

7. Cover pot And simmer for 45 minutes to 1 houror until the vent is fork tender.

8. Drink Stew in bowls brown rice or include rice to shellfish, if wanted. (Rice not included in clinical evaluation.)

NUTRITIONAL VALUES

Serving size: 1/4 of recipe, not like rice

Calories: 308

Carbohydrate: 25 g

Fat: 7 g (2 g saturated)

Protein: 33 g

Cholesterol: 84 mg

Sodium: 414 mg

Fiber: 6 g

Asian Chicken Lettuce Wraps Recipe

Weight Management & Bariatrics

SERVINGS: 4

INGREDIENTS

1 can (8 oz) bamboo shoots, drained and minced

1 can (8 oz) water chestnuts, drained and minced

3 tbsp sherry cooking wine

2 tbsp hoisin sauce

1 tbsp unsalted peanut butter

2 tsp low-sodium soy sauce

2 tsp hot pepper sauce, like Sriracha

2 packs (.035 ounce each) sugar replacement (such as Splenda)

1 tbsp minced garlic

1 cup minced onion

1/2 pound ground chicken breast

1 tsp minced ginger

1/4 tsp salt

1 tsp toasted sesame oil

8 little leaves butter lettuce

1 whole green onion, chopped

1 small cucumber, seeded and chopped into 1" strips

DIRECTIONS

1. In a Medium bowlcombine the bamboo shoots water chestnuts, sherry, hoisin sauce, peanut butter, soy sauce, hot-pepper sauce, and sugar replacement. Mix well. Put aside.

2. Mist a Large, nonstick skillet with cooking spray and place over moderate heat.

3. Insert the Onion and cook for 4 minutes or until onions are aromatic and simmer.

4. Insert the Garlic and cook for a minute longer.

5. Boost the warmth to medium-high and include the ground poultry, ginger, and salt.

6. Cook, Dividing the chicken using a spatula or wooden spoon, for 3 to 4 minutes, until no longer pink.

7. Insert the Bamboo take and water chestnut mix.

8. Cook for Two minutes, or till heated through.

9. Stir in The eucalyptus oil.

10. Eliminate the pan from the heat.

11. To function, Split the chicken mix evening on every one of the carrot leaves.

12. Top with Chopped green onion and pineapple. Drink immediately.

NUTRITIONAL VALUES

Serving size: 2 lettuces wraps

Calories: 155

Cholesterol: 33 mg

Carbohydrates: 11 g

Sodium: 637 mg

Fat: 4 g

Protein: 16 g

Dietary Fiber: 5 g

Sugar: 4 g

Chicken Cheesesteak Wrap Recipe

Weight Management & Bariatrics

SERVINGS: 1)

INGREDIENTS

1/4 pound boneless, skinless chicken breast cut of visible fat

1/4 cup onions, chopped

1/4 cup green pepper, sliced

1/4 cup mushrooms, sliced

1 liter (3/4 oz) Laughing Cow Original light swiss cheese Or equal

1 whole wheat germ, low-carb tortilla

2 tsp sliced pickled hot chili peppers (optional)

DIRECTIONS

1. Place Chicken breast cutting board, lb to 1/4" lean and slice into very thin strips.

2. Put a Skillet over medium high heat and peppermint with cooking spray.

3. Insert the Onion and poultry to the skillet and cook till onions are translucent and chicken is no longer pink during.

4. Insert green Peppers and mushrooms into the pan and cook until mushrooms and peppers soften.

5. Place Tortilla between two moist paper towels. Microwave for 20 minutes.

6. Lay the Warm tortilla level and spread cheese within an even strip at the center.

7. Top with Chicken, peppers, mushrooms and onions.

8. Add chili Peppers when using.

9. Twist Sides of tortilla over centre. Drink immediately.

NUTRITIONAL VALUES

Serving size: 1 wrap

Calories: 264

Carbohydrate: 17 g

Fat: 6 g (2 g saturated)

Protein: 33 g

Cholesterol: 76 mg

Sodium: 620 mg

Fiber: 4 g

Not Truly Fried Rice Recipe

Weight Management & Bariatrics

SERVINGS: 2

INGREDIENTS

2 tbsp low-sodium soy sauce

1 tsp mustard

1 tsp chili paste

1 tsp toasted sesame oil

3 oz boneless, skinless chicken breast cut into 1/2" cubes

Black pepper, to taste

1/2 cup finely chopped entire green onions

1/4 cup sliced lettuce

1 tsp garlic, minced

3/4 cup cooked short-grain brown rice

1/4 cup frozen peas

2 large egg whites

Olive oil spray

DIRECTIONS

1. In a Small bowl, mix soy sauce, mustard, chili paste and sesame oil. Put aside.

2. Season The cubed chicken with pepper.

3. Mist a Big, nonstick wok or skillet with cooking spray and set over medium high heat until it's hot enough to get a drop of water to sizzle on it.

4. Scatter The chicken cubes to the wok or skillet.

5. Cook, Stirring occasionally, until browned on all sides and no longer pink inside.

6. Transfer chicken to a plate and cover to keep warm.

7. Gently Mist the wok or skillet with cooking spray . Place over medium-high heat.

8. Insert the Green lettuce, onions, and garlic into the pan.

9. Cook, Stirring often, for 2-3 minutes.

10. Insert the Cooked peas and rice.

11. Continue Cooking and stirring for two minutes until the mix is hot throughout.

12. Employing a Spoon or spatula, make a hole in the veggies and rice to expose the middle of the pan.

13. Off the Warmth, gently mist the exposed portion of this pan with cooking spray.

14. Insert the Egg whites and stir to combine them in the rice.

15. Cook for 1-2 seconds, or until the egg is totally cooked.

16. Return the Chicken into the pan and stir in the fried soy sauce mixture.

17. Leave Heat, stirring constantly, for about 1 minute or till heated. Drink immediately.

NUTRITIONAL VALUES

Serving size: 1/2 recipe

Calories: 208

Carbohydrate: 25 g

Fat: 3.5 g (1 g saturated)

Protein: 17 g

Cholesterol: 25 mg

Sodium: 260 mg

Fiber: 3.5 g

Egg-Chilada Recipe

Weight Management & Bariatrics

SERVINGS: 1)

INGREDIENTS

1 egg 1 egg white

Black pepper and salt to taste

1 oz protein of choice (poultry, tofu, or ground beef work well)

2 tbsp salsa (Including Tostito's moderate)

1 tbsp shredded Mexican blend cheese

2 tbsp plain fat-free Greek yogurt

DIRECTIONS

1. Scramble the egg and egg in a small bowl

2. Spray a Skillet or griddle with cooking spray and put it on medium heat.

3. Pour the Scrambled eggs on the skillet and permit it to disperse into a generally round shape.

4. Leave the Eggs for a moment or 2; allowing the borders to place. Add a dab of black pepper and salt to the eggs while they are placing.

5. Slide a Spatula under the eggs and reverse (do not worry if a few egg pops off at this stage).

6. Cook eggs On the opposite side about 2 minutes until fully cooked and move to a plate.

7. Create a Strip of filling to your egg-chilada using 1 ounce. Protein of choice and Mexican cheese.

8. Roll up The egg"pancake" to shape your egg-chilada.

9. Top with Steak and Greek yogurt.

NUTRITIONAL VALUES

Serving size: 1 egg-chilada

Calories: 171

Carbohydrate: 3 g

Fat: 8 g

Protein: 23 g

Sodium: 432 mg

Sugar: 3 g

Cheesecake Pudding Recipe

Weight Management & Bariatrics

INGREDIENTS

1 cup plain skillet Greek yogurt

1 bundle sugar-free cheesecake pudding mix

DIRECTIONS

1. Blend ingredients in a blender and puree until smooth.

NUTRITIONAL VALUES

Serving size: 1/4 cup

Protein: 7 g

Pan-Fried Rainbow Trout Recipe

Weight Management & Bariatrics

SERVINGS: 2

INGREDIENTS

8 oz rainbow trout fillets

3 Tbsp yellow cornmeal

1 1/3 Tbsp chopped parsley

1/4 tsp ground celery seeds

1/4 teaspoon ground black pepper

1 pinch salt

2 teaspoon olive oil

DIRECTIONS

1. Clean and Scrub fish fillets. Check to be certain all bones have been removed. Pat dry.

2. Mix together cornmeal, salt, pepper, celery seed and chopped parsley.

3. Cover Fish using cornmeal mix and press on fish.

4. Heating Olive oil in skillet. Cook 2 to 3 minutes each side. Fish ought to be brown and sharp and should flake out when pierced with a fork.

NUTRITIONAL ANALYSIS PER SERVING (4 oz serving)

Serving Size: About 1 cup

Calories: 240

Total Fat: 10g

Complete Protein: 25g

Total Carbohydrates: 10g

Cholesterol: 67mg

Sodium: 338mg

Sugars: 0g

Pumpkin and Black Bean Soup Recipe

Weight Management & Bariatrics

SERVINGS: 6 (about 1 cup per day)

35 minutes

INGREDIENTS

2 tbsp olive oil

1 medium onion, chopped

4 garlic cloves, minced

1 tbsp ground cumin

1 tsp chili powder

1/2 tsp black pepper

2 cans (15 oz) black beans, rinsed and drained

1 cup canned diced tomatoes

2 cups beef broth

1 can (16 oz) pumpkin puree

DIRECTIONS

1. Heat oil In a soup pot over medium heat, sauté garlic, onions, cumin, chili powder and pepper till tender.

2. Stir in Black beans, tomatoes, broth and pumpkin.

3. Simmer Discovered stirring occasionally for approximately 25 minutes before soup is really a thick consistency

4. Drink as Can be or puree with an immersion blender to get a smooth consistency.

SUGGESTIONS

Stir in plain Greek yogurt for additional protein and creaminess.

Insert 1/2-pound ground beef for a further protein.

NUTRITIONAL ANALYSIS PER SERVING

Serving Size: About 1 cup

Calories: 290

Total Fat: 6g

Complete Protein: 15g

Total Carbohydrates: 46g

Dietary Fiber: 11g

Sugars: 3g

Asian Pork Tenderloin Recipe

Weight Management & Bariatrics

SERVINGS: 8

INGREDIENTS

1/3 cup light soy sauce

1/3 cup brown sugar

2 tbsp Worcestershire sauce

2 tbsp lemon juice

2 tbsp rice vinegar

1 tbsp dry mustard

1 tbsp ginger

1 1/2 tsp pepper

4 garlic cloves or ready minced

2 pounds pork tenderloin

DIRECTIONS

1. Mix Ingredients together in freezer-safe bag.

2. Place tenderloin in freezer bag and rub marinade on pork.

3. Refrigerate Overnight or put in freezer for future use.

4. Bake for 30-40 minutes in 375º F levels OR prepare slow cooker on low for 4-6 hours.

NUTRITIONAL ANALYSIS PER SERVING

Serving Size: About 4 oz

Calories: 256

Total Fat: 9g

Total Carbohydrates: 9g

Dietary Fiber: 0g

Sugars: 8g

Sodium: 658 mg

Complete Protein: 34g

RECOMMENDATION

Some individuals have trouble tolerating dense meats such as Beef and pork following surgery. You will bear these meats when they're cooked slowly and at a moist cooking supply such as a toaster. You may serve this pork with a side of vegetables that are cooked. Attempt cooked cabbage with Asian seasonings.

Greek Yogurt Chicken Recipe

Weight Management & Bariatrics

SERVINGS: 4

INGREDIENTS

4 boneless skinless chicken breasts (4 ounces each)

1 cup plain Greek yogurt

1/2 cup grated Parmesan cheese

1 tsp garlic powder

1 1/2 tsp seasoning salt

1/2 tsp pepper

DIRECTIONS

1. Preheat Oven to 375 degrees.

2. Blend Greek yogurt, sausage and cheese in bowl.

3. Line Baking sheet with foil and spray with cooking spray.

4. Coat each Chicken breast in Greek yogurt mix and set on foiled baking sheet.

5. Bake for 45 minutes.

NUTRITIONAL ANALYSIS PER SERVING

Total Calories: 266

Total fat: 4g

Saturated Fat: 3g

Total Carbohydrates: 3g

Dietary Fiber: 0g

Sugars: 2g

Protein: 46g

High-Protein Cottage Cheese Pancakes Recipe

Weight Management & Bariatrics

SERVINGS: 4 pancakes

INGREDIENTS

1/3 cup all-purpose flour

1/2 tsp baking soda

1 cup low-fat cottage cheese

1/2 tbsp olive oil

3 eggs, lightly beaten

DIRECTIONS

1. Blend Flour and baking soda in a little bowl.

2. Blend Remaining ingredients in a big bowl.

3. Pour Flour mix to cottage cheese mixture and stir fry until just incorporated.

4. Heat a Large skillet over moderate heat, coat with cooking spray.

5. Pour? Cup pieces of batter onto skillet and cook until bubbles appear on the surface.

6. Flip and Cook on the other side until brown.

7. Drink with low sugar. (Attempt Walden Farms.)

NUTRITIONAL ANALYSIS PER SERVING

Serving Size: 1 pancake

Calories: 152

Carbohydrate: 10 g

Fat: 7 grams

Protein: 13 g

Sodium: 385 mg

Sugar: 2 g

Spicy Deviled Eggs Recipe

Weight Management & Bariatrics

SERVINGS: 3

INGREDIENTS

6 hard-boiled eggs (You won't use three of those yolks in this recipe.)

Two Tablespoons of creamy horseradish sauce or Greek yogurt

1/2 tsp dill

1/4 tsp hot mustard (Utilize Dijon for moderate deviled eggs)

⅛ tsp salt

Dash of black pepper and paprika

DIRECTIONS

1. Peel the eggs and cut in half lengthwise.

2. Place 3 Yolks into a mixing bowl and set the whites aside. (Save another few yolks for another use.)

3. Mash the Yolks with creamy horseradish sauce or Greek yogurt, dill, salt and mustard.

4. Spoon or Pipe filling into egg white halves.

5. Sprinkle With pepper and paprika.

NUTRITIONAL ANALYSIS PER SERVING

Serving Size: 2 deviled eggs

Calories: 131

Fat: 8.7 g

Protein: 10 g

Carbohydrate: 1 g

Cholesterol: 225 mg

Sodium: 219 mg

Sugar: 0 g

Slow-Cooker Chicken Taco Filling Recipe

Weight Management & Bariatrics

SERVINGS: 4

INGREDIENTS

16 oz (1 pound) skinless, boneless chicken breasts

1 cup chicken broth

1 (1.25 ounce) package dry taco seasoning mix

INSTRUCTIONS

1. Mix Chicken broth and taco seasoning in a bowl.

2. Place Chicken breast in toaster.

3. Pour Broth and seasoning mix over chicken.

4. Cover and Cook for 6-8 hours.

5. Shred chicken.

6. Cook Low for extra 30 minutes to consume excess juices.

7. Drink as Filling for tacos, topping for a salad or alone to get a protein resource.

NUTRITION FACTS (1 serving, 4 oz)

Calories: 148

Total Fat: 2.4 gram

Total Carbohydrates: 6 g

Sugars: 0 grams

Protein: 23 g

Sodium: 930 milligrams (use low sodium broth and seasonings to Reduce sodium content)

Ginger Beef Stir Fry Recipe

Weight Management & Bariatrics

SERVINGS: 6

INGREDIENTS

1 lb flank steak (cut into 1/4-inch strips)

2 tsp ground ginger

2 medium garlic cloves

6 oz beef broth (fat free)

1/4 cup (2 oz) hoisin sauce

3 tbsp soy sauce

1 tbsp cornstarch

1 tsp canola oil

1/4 tsp crushed red pepper flakes

3 oz broccoli florets

1/2 medium yellow, green or red bell pepper cut into strips

1/2 cup instant brown rice

2 medium stalks bok choy cut to 1/2-inch pieces

8-ounce can chopped water chestnuts

INSTRUCTIONS

1. In blending Bowl, stir together beef, ginger and garlic. Put aside.

2. Prepare Rice according to instructions on package.

3. Blend broth, hoisin sauce, soy sauce and cornstarch in a bowl. Stir until dissolved.

4. In wok or Skillet, warm oil and red pepper flakes over medium-high warmth.

5. Cook Beef 4-5 minutes or till browned. Stir constantly. Put aside.

6. Place Broccoli, bell pepper and lettuce into pan. Cook medium-high heat for 2-3 minutes or till tender-crisp. Stir. (If mixture gets too dry, add 1-2 tablespoons water)

7. Stir in bok choy and water chestnuts. Cook for extra 1-2 minutes or beneath bok choy is tender-crisp. Stir constantly.

8. Create a Well in middle of pan, and pour broth.

9. Cook 1-2 Minutes until broth thickens, sometimes stir fry.

10. Mix in beef. Cook 1-2 minutes until warm.

11. Serve over rice.

NUTRITION FACTS (⅙ recipe)

Calories: 275

Fat: 8 g

Carbohydrates: 25 g

Dietary Fiber: 2 g

Sugars: 6 g

Protein: 17 g

Classic Hummus Recipe

Weight Management & Bariatrics

SERVINGS: 12

INGREDIENTS

1 teaspoon garlic, crushed and peeled

1 15-ounce can chickpeas, rinsed

3 tbsp fresh lemon juice

3 tbsp extra-virgin olive oil

1 tbsp tahini

1/2 tsp salt

INSTRUCTIONS

1. In food Chip, chop garlic until finely minced.

2. Scrape down the sides of food processor and include chickpeas, lemon juice, oil, tahini, and salt.

3. Procedure Until completely smooth, scraping down sides as required (1-2 minutes).

NUTRITION FACTS (2 tbsp)

Calories: 72

Fat: 4.5 g

Protein: 1.5 g

Carbohydrate: 7.5 g

Cholesterol: 0 milligrams

Sodium: 149 mg

Sugar: 0 g

Chapter 2 Cosmetic Surgery Gains besides Helping You Shed Weight

You would likely eat less if you felt full after ingesting a Small quantity of food. That is what regular surgery does and it helps people eliminate weight.

Bariatric surgery enhances weight reduction in obese Men and Women that Haven't attained long-term success along with other weight loss efforts. Bariatric surgery reduces the gut's storage capacity, which restricts food intake and can help you feel full much sooner than usual.

But there is more than 1 kind of bariatric surgery. Alternatives include gastric bypass, sleeve gastrectomy, gastric banding and gastric plication. Your doctor will help determine if you are a candidate and, if so, which option will work best for you personally.

"If You've Got a body mass index (BMI) of 35 or more, then this Means you probably need to shed over 65 pounds," says bariatric surgery nurse Karen Schulz, MSN, CNS, CBN. Without making modifications, you can develop critical health problems due to the extra weight. Virtually all individuals with a BMI of 40 or more are candidates for the surgery.

Dietary alterations after bariatric surgery

Together with their stomachs, individuals who've had the surgery need to eat really slowly and take little bites. "Some of the most difficult adjustments for patients is they can't drink liquids while eating. Patients must drink their fluids at least 30 minutes before or 30 minutes after ingestion, but it does not take long for most people to fix," Ms. Schulz states.

People who've experienced the surgery also take vitamins and Supplements recommended by a nutritionist who counsels patients following the procedure.

Weight reduction Just One health benefit of several

Bariatric surgery offers people considerable and continuing Weight reduction.

"Most folks who need to shed 65 or more pounds have attempted numerous times to eliminate the weight by themselves. While they might have some success initially, less than 5% of individuals keep the weight off for five years or longer," says bariatric physician and Manager of Cleveland Clinic's Bariatric and Metabolic Institute Philip Schauer, MD... In reality, he states they generally add the weight back in under a year.

Losing weight and gaining back it does nothing to Mitigate the possible health issues related to obesity. You have to continue to keep off the weight for no less than five years to think about the reduction a victory and one which may lead to a happier, healthier you.

Advantages of continuing weight loss through routine surgery include:

1. Long-term Remission for type two diabetes. "A current Cleveland Clinic study indicates that bariatric surgery induces long-term remission of difficult-to-control type two diabetes.

The outcomes of the study reveal the procedure is extremely successful for overweight patients with type 2 diabetes, enabling virtually all patients to stay free of insulin and also adjunct drugs for at least three years post surgery," states Dr. Schauer.

2. Enriched cardiovascular wellness. Weight reduction surgery reduces a individual's risk of coronary heart disease, stroke and peripheral heart disease. "Blood pressure and cholesterol levels may go back to normal or near normal after surgery, decreasing the dangers and enhancing general well-being," Ms. Schulz states.

3. Relief of depression. Many overweight men and women feel miserable due to bad body image and social stigma. Even younger individuals who take substantial excess fat find it hard to take part in activities they might otherwise like, resulting in social isolation and depression. Losing this extra weight may improve psychological health in these patients.

4. Remove Obstructive sleep apnea. Achieving and sustaining a more normal weight range frequently allows individuals with sleep apnea to quit having a CPAP device at bedtime.

5. Joint Pain relief. Carrying around excess weight puts a great deal of strain in your own back joints, often causing chronic pain and joint damage. "The sustained and significant weight loss

that happens after bariatric surgery alleviates the strain on joints and frequently permits people to quit using pain medicines and enjoy considerably more freedom," Dr. Schauer states.

6. Boost Fertility. Weight loss surgery may also boost fertility throughout childbearing years.

7. Alleviate other health ailments. Weight loss surgery may relieve metabolic syndrome, pregnancy disorders, gallbladder disease and much more.

Together with obesity and its related health complications increasing in an alarming rate in the usa, bariatric surgery surely signifies a highly effective tool for supplying sustained relief for obese men and women.

Sleeve Gastrectomy--a minimally invasive surgery to decrease the dimensions of the gut --is currently the hottest weight loss surgery at our Center and on earth. Columbia physician Dr. Abraham Krikhely informs how it helps patients reach their desired goals--improving both the health and quality of life.

What's a sleeve gastrectomy?

At a sleeve gastrectomy, a Part of the gut is eliminated To create the stomach smaller -- about the shape and size of a banana. It's a surgery that people frequently perform minimally invasively. Working with a TV display, we utilize small camera and instruments, inserted through some tiny incisions. Having a smaller tummy, patients consume less. Additionally, the surgery is related to hormone fluctuations that lead to diminished appetite.

Why is this surgery the favored choice by a lot of?

People often see the Fantastic achievement that their buddies and Family members have experienced with the entire sleeve then need exactly the very same effects.

Patients achieve dependable weight loss using a straightforward operation they can easily understand. It is reasonable that using a little tummy, you may eat less and lose more fat.

The sleeve gastrectomy has been found to be more Effective compared to gastric band and doesn't require positioning of a foreign device or needle alterations that the band does. It's also nearly as powerful as a gastric bypass that has some long-term dangers the sleeve does not have.

What are the advantages?

Normally, patients lose about 60-70percent of the excess weight. Many studies also have proven that sleeve gastrectomy is extremely capable of treating and causing the remission of diabetes, diabetes, higher blood pressure and other medical conditions related to morbid obesity. Patients report greater confidence and energy and are happy to have the ability to participate in more activities.

How long does the surgery take and how quickly is the Retrieval?

A sleeve gastrectomy takes approximately one hour to finish and Usually entails a night or 2 at the hospital.

The recovery is rather fast. We expect our patients to be Up and around instantly. Most are walking daily following surgery. Initially, there might be some pain across the incisions but that is treated with pain medication and normally resolves in a couple of days.

Just how much patients return to work is determined by how much Physical action is necessary. My basic rule is not any heavy lifting for a month following surgery. People who have desk jobs typically return to work after two or three weeks.

Is there some particular follow up required?

Continuing follow-up together with our staff is what enables our patients To attain such fantastic results with fewer complications.

It Is Essential to have regular testing of this vitamin Levels within your body to ensure you are getting the vitamins and nutrients you want. In addition, we urge surveillance endoscopies on a regular basis, to be sure everything is functioning properly and check for signs of reflux--a state in which the contents of the stomach or intestines back up into the esophagus. Some individuals can develop reflux following sleeve gastrectomy, therefore we see them very carefully. In addition, we perform our surgery in a means that's considered to reduce this risk.

Reflux is generally treatable with drugs, yet some Patients might require a gastric bypass. Another, newer alternative qualified for effective therapy for reflux and being analyzed particularly for the sleeve gastrectomy is LINX, a magnetic device that resembles a necklace that's surgically placed around the sidewalk. The beads sit round the esophagus and also keep acid from coming up into it. When a person swallows, the beads different and permit the food to return. They remainder of the time that the beads remain shut, preventing backflow or damage to the lining of the esophagus.

What Type of weight reduction can you expect out of a sleeve Gastrectomy and can it be lasting?

Thus Far, We've seen great lasting weight reduction, of approximately 60-70% at the short term. Studies reveal long-term weight loss after 5-10 years to be approximately 50-60percent of their patient's excess fat. But these are only the averages -- do not allow the figures hold you back. Some individuals do better. Believe in yourself. The best way to change how you live your life following the surgery may have a massive effect. I recently operated to a 23 year-old man who weighed 424 pounds, using a BMI 68, also could not lose enough pounds during exercise and diet. Annually following a sleeve gastrectomy, he lost almost 200 pounds and plans to join the military, a long-held aim. As a physician, I am deeply moved by men and women that can satisfy their fantasies, and completely enjoy their lifestyles.

Which Are the Most Common Post-Op Risks and Side Effects Connected with Cosmetic Surgery?

Some bariatric surgery dangers include:

- Acid reflux

- Anesthesia-related Dangers

- Persistent Nausea and vomiting

- Dilation of esophagus

- Inability To eat specific foods

- Infection

- Obstruction Of gut

- Weight Gain or failure to get rid of weight

Bariatric Surgery Long-Term Hazards

Bariatric surgery includes some long term dangers for patients, Such as:

- Dumping Syndrome, a disease which could result in symptoms such as nausea and dizziness

- Low blood sugar

- Malnutrition

- Vomiting

- Ulcers

- Bowel Obstruction

- Hernias

Summary of Bariatric Surgery Risks and Complications by Process

Risks and side effects change from regular process. The Following list isn't comprehensive, but briefly summarizes risks of gastric bypass and gastric sleeve.

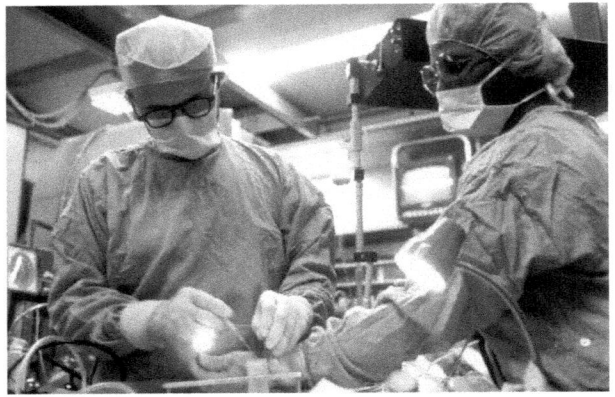

Your surgeon will Make Certain You Realize that the Dangers and complications of your particular procedure.

Risks of Gastric Bypass:

- Breakage

- Dumping Infection

- Gallstones (hazard increases with quick or

Substantial weight reduction)

- Hernia

- Internal Infection or profuse bleeding of this

Surgical wound

- Leakage

- Perforation Of intestines or stomach

- Pouch/anastomotic Obstruction or bowel obstruction

- Protein or vitamin malnutrition

- Pulmonary And/or cardiac problems

- Skin Care separation

- Spleen or Other organ harm

- Stomach Or intestine ulceration

- Stricture

- Vitamin Or iron deficiency

Risks of Gastric Sleeve:

- Blood Infection

- Gallstones (hazard increases with quick or

Substantial weight reduction)

- Hernia

- Internal Infection or profuse bleeding of this

Surgical wound

- Leakage

- Perforation Of intestines or stomach

- Skin Care separation

- Stricture

- Vitamin or iron deficiency

Reduce Your Bariatric Surgery Hazards

You can help lower a Few of the dangers and possible side Consequences by:

- Decreasing Your Own Body Mass Index (BMI)

- Growing your level of exercise

- Stopping Smoking

Our Presurgical Lifestyle Plan can help you prepare yourself for bariatric surgery.

What's recovery following surgery like?

Immediately after your surgery, you'll probably remain Overnight in the hospital or surgical centre for a few days. Your stomach will most likely feel sore and might be swollen, which means you may get medicine to lower your discomfort.

During this period, your vital signs (for example your heartbeat, your blood pressure along with your respiration) will be tracked, and you're going to be assessed to make sure that you're experiencing some post-surgery complications.

Before you leave the clinic, the surgical team will give you comprehensive instructions about the best way best to prevent complications. You will also be advised as soon as you're able to resume particular activities and the way you're eating program Need to change. If possible, have a friend or relative present to take Notes and ask questions. Once you're discharged, do not hesitate to telephone your Physician's office should you have any queries or concerns.

What can you expect in your short term recovery?

The following are some important elements associated with your Short term retrieval, in addition to suggestions to ensure that your recovery spreads easily:

Request assistance if you need it

It may Be Hard to Manage your duties around the home in the immediate wake of your surgery, so request help from relatives or friends if you require it. You might also need to appear into briefly earning hired help.

Practice your new eating plan

Throughout the first six months following surgery, your basic lines will be all that is holding your brand new sleeve together, therefore it is crucial that you follow your eating plan and also provide these basic lines an opportunity to properly cure.

You will drink clear fluids for the first day following surgery and will probably be set on a liquid-only diet for the first week or so. Following that, you will transition into tender pureed foods for 2 weeks. It is extremely important that you don't transition into solid foods too soon, since this might harm your gut and result in side effects like nausea, vomiting and stomach cramps.

For the first fourteen days following surgery, you'll need to Limit to an intake of approximately 400 calories. This might have been daunting prior to your operation, but on account of the gastric sleeve surgery you may now obviously have diminished appetite that may make it simpler for you to devote to the limited portion sizes. Since your body adjusts to the decreased variety of calories while your recuperate from the surgery, you might feel more tired than normal, but do not worry: After you start to slowly consume more calories, you are going to feel that your energy returning.

Give yourself time before resuming normal activities

Take at least fourteen days to recuperate after your surgery before You return to work, particularly in the event that you've got a physically demanding occupation.

Walking as soon as possible following surgery will help stop Deep vein thrombosis, which can be a potentially harmful condition which occurs when a blood clot forms in a vein deep in the body. Your physician might even motivate you to walk the moment a couple of hours after surgery.

Nevertheless, give yourself time to Recuperate and do not do too much too soon. Bear in mind, you might realize that you become tired faster than normal. Even though you can gradually increase your level of cardiovascular exercise, you need to wait at least four months following surgery until you do any weightlifting or other kinds of exceptionally strenuous activity. Overexerting yourself might result in a hernia growing on your surgical wound, which occurs when muscle, inner tissue or a portion of the stomach pokes through the healing procedure.

Work through short term emotional Results

You need to expect to possibly experience some disposition Changes as the body adjusts to fewer calories. Remember this is a typical psychological complication that will probably pass quite quickly.

Think about your long-term healing?

Obtaining gastric sleeve surgery impacts not only what you consume But also how that you eat for the rest of your life. It's necessary that you understand that while getting surgery is a terrific starting point, you will also have to make different adjustments to get--and stay--as wholesome as you can.

These tips Can Help You prepare for and browse your post-surgery life:

Stick with your new eating plan

You are going to need to significantly alter How You eat after Your surgery, which will probably be a massive alteration. Here's a Brief list of the modifications you can expect:

• Eat quite gradually

• Eat just Small amounts of food at one time, and remember your new gut is a lot smaller

• Chew thoroughly and do not consume your food until after you've completely hauled it to some mashed consistency

• Do not consume and drink at exactly the exact same time, since this may lead to food to move throughout your new tummy too fast; rather, drink a drink about 30 minutes before you eat a meal

Get busy

When your surgeon provides you the OK, you should Begin a Post-surgery workout program. Not only can this be a significant part keeping off the weight that you lose, it will also reduce your total proportion of body fat. Additionally, getting active will ease your adjustment to life following surgery and raise your energy.

Take vitamins and nutritional supplements

Even though your system will still absorb nutrients following your Surgery, it is going to be receiving much fewer calories than before--in the end; you are going to be eating less food. Your health care provider will inform you just what vitamins and nutritional supplements you need to take, but you will probably need a range of multivitamins in addition to other doses of B vitamins.

Meet with a dietitian

As you'll be taking in less food, it is even more significant to make healthful choices that lead to you getting as much food-based nourishment as possible. A dietitian can help you invent and maintain a healthful eating strategy with time.

Your Physician will Tell You just how many calories you need to Be getting, which will almost certainly be approximately 900 to 1,000 calories every day in six months post-surgery. Be aware that eating foods or drinking beverages that are high in calories, fat or sugar ought to be avoided.

Maintain your followup appointments with your Physician

You will need to place and maintain followup appointments with your Physician to make certain you're recovering nicely and progressing as you ought to after your surgery. Through these appointments, you are able to ask questions and discuss concerns about your diet, exercise, weight loss and mental recovery. Likewise, your health care provider can determine that you are on the ideal path and indicate any necessary alterations to maximize your healing.

Prepare yourself for longer-term psychological Results

You clearly expect your body to alter after gastric Sleeve surgery, but do not neglect the emotional side of this equation.

First off, you might discover that you crave unhealthy foods, which is stressful. Joining a support group for gastric sleeve patients can allow you to adapt for this and other modifications you might be experiencing, and also locating a therapist with experience in counselling weight loss patients might be valuable also.

Additionally, Know about the fact that a Number of the Activities you enjoyed with friends might no longer be sensible for you post-surgery. You will still have the ability to interact, but you will want to get it done in a much healthier manner. As an instance, if you are utilized to going out to dinner with friends or with drinks with your colleagues after work, why don't you find some new and more physiological actions to talk about? Consider starting a walking group in dinner or ask your friends to match for a bicycle ride or a hike rather than post-work dinner and beverages. Odds are good they'll welcome the opportunity to pick up some wholesome habits themselves!

While you may experience some favorable emotional Results As you eliminate fat and assume a larger role in caring for yourself and keeping your weight loss, you could also experience feelings of melancholy. Remember that although becoming gastric sleeve surgery can definitely prompt remarkable life changes in certain respects, so it won't fix every one of your troubles, and it is unrealistic to presume that you won't experience several periods of feeling down or using low self-esteem.

Additionally, you're Family and Friends may respond to you differently as you shed weight, and a few could even attempt to sabotage your weight loss efforts. It can Be Hard to adjust to This Kind of response, which can be Still another reason post-surgery counselling and joining a support group can Be really beneficial.

Conclusion

Bariatric surgery is a means to alter the total amount of food your stomach can hold or the way that your body absorbs nourishment and calories, leading to weight reduction. There are a range of different techniques to carry out the surgery. Virtually all processes are done laparoscopically, a method that reduces incision size and reduces recovery time and discomfort. Your physician can allow you to decide which procedure is ideal for you.

Our surgeons have performed thousands of procedures and use a group of caregivers to help you along your weight loss clinic, from choosing to have surgery to preparing for surgery and adapting to a different way of life and wellness after surgery. The group comprises:

Intake Coordinators who assist with scheduling, insurance verification and queries on the Way

Experienced surgeons

Devoted bariatric surgery nurses

Registered dietitians who specialize in bariatric surgery patients

Psychologists trained to give advice to bariatric surgery patients

Dedicated bariatric surgery inpatient unit

Exercise group concentrated on the severely obese - a part unique to our schedule

CPSIA information can be obtained
at www.ICGtesting.com
Printed in the USA
BVHW041643070221
599576BV00005B/470